Finding My F**king Unicorn

The Workbook

No part of this publication may be reproduced, stored in a retrieval system, or transmitted in any form or by any means without the prior permission of the publishers and copyright owner.

First published in Great Britain by Labradorite Press

An imprint of Not From This Planet

Copyright © 2023 Michelle Gordon
Illustrations © 2023 Amanda Bigrell
Cover Design by Lucja Fratczak-Kay & The Amethyst Angel

The rights of Michelle Gordon to be identified as the author of this work have been asserted in accordance with the Copyright, Designs and Patents Act 1988, Sections 77 and 78.

The publishers and author can accept no legal responsibility for any consequences arising from the application of information, advice or instruction given in this publication. They also make no promises or assurances of your life improving if you act upon the information and guidance within.

Finding My F**king Unicorn

The Workbook

Michelle Gordon

```
Also by Michelle Gordon:
```

Fiction:
The Girl Who Loved Too Much

Earth Angel Series:
The Earth Angel Training Academy
The Earth Angel Awakening
The Other Side
The Twin Flame Reunion
The Twin Flame Retreat
The Twin Flame Resurrection
The Twin Flame Reality
The Twin Flame Rebellion
The Twin Flame Reignition
The Twin Flame Resolution
The Old Soul's Handbook

Visionary Collection
Heaven dot com
The Doorway to PAM
The Elphite
I'm Here

The Magical Doorway Series
The Magical Faerie Door
The Magical Mermaid Portal
The Magical Dragon Mirror

Non-fiction:
Where's My F**king Unicorn?

Poetry:
Duelling Poets

Praise for
WHERE'S MY F**KING UNICORN?

This is a beautiful, light hearted book! I love it.- Genna

Light-hearted and motivational, we all need a little bit of this magical book in our lives!- Rachel

Love love love this book! Simple yet full of non judgemental inspiration. Sharing with ALL my friends so we can go Unicorn riding together. - Jenny

The concise messages in this book summarise beautifully all that is needed to make positive changes in life.- Arcaya

This book is a funny and good read. If you are looking for a laugh and taking a break from being so serious about life, this is a good book.- Jennifer

Simple, to the point, reader friendly, relatable. This book speaks to you, it was exactly the inspiration I needed at the moment.- Stefania

What a little gem of a book. Inspiring yet down to earth at the same time. Well worth a read if you need a little kick up the bum.- Becki

Loved it. Thought it was witty, an easy read and a great reminder to be unapologetically you.- Betty

Cute. Short. Actionable. - Jessica

For all my fellow Unicorn seekers out there -
keep sparkling like the fucking superstars you are!

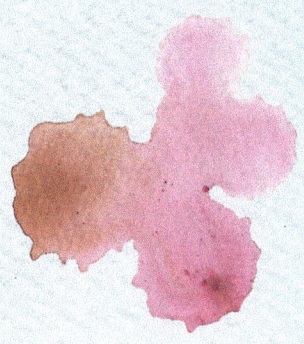

Introduction

In late September 2016, I woke up one Saturday morning with words running through my mind, words that I then scribbled down in my journal, which over the course of a weekend, I fleshed out into the format of a short book.

That book was

WHERE'S MY F**KING UNICORN?

A year later, the Unicorn in all its shiny glory was available in bookstores, airports, independent retailers and funky card shops. A few months after that, the Unicorn had gone global, and people were posting pictures of it on Instagram and saying how much they loved it.

Did I have any idea how my life would change from writing those words down?

Of course not. Not a fucking clue.

And in truth, though much has changed, mostly for the better, I have still experienced some of the worst moments of my life since then. So finding your Unicorn doesn't necessarily change everything so that every day is filled with rainbows and glitter, but it does make things a bit more colourful. (Even if it's only your language…)

In those few years, I realised that though many readers took the advice and ran with it (making changes in their lives and finally nabbing those Unicorns) simply knowing the reasons why your life sucks doesn't help everyone to take action. So I developed a simple process that helps you to work out which Unicorn you would like to focus on, and how to take action to move towards it.

After running this as a workshop in person and online, I have seen how it can work for others and would like to share it now with you.

BECAUSE YOU ARE A FUCKING SUPERSTAR WHO DESERVES TO EXPERIENCE RIDING YOUR UNICORNS.

Now, if you're anything like me, you will often pick up a 'how-to' book, read it from start to finish, think it's great, will really help, but never actually go through it properly and do the exercises.

In order to stop you from doing that, I have created this book in the format of a workbook, which means that there are actual spaces for you to fill in, not just for the one Unicorn, but for several.

So please actually do the exercises, because that's the only way you will experience anything changing in your life. Simply reading this book will not change your life!

I repeat:

READING THIS BOOK WILL NOT CHANGE YOUR LIFE.

But taking the ACTIONS described in this book MIGHT.

Before We Begin the Unicorn Hunt

Buddy Up

To help you on this mad adventure, I highly recommend finding a buddy who also wants to chase Unicorns. Sometimes, it's hard to see our own blocks, our excuses, and our fears. It might be easier for a friend (or even a complete stranger, if your friends are too nice) to point out where you are stumbling, and what your resistances are to making changes.

You could ask a friend, or reach out to someone in a group of like-minded people online. I would recommend perhaps not asking a family member, unless you are very open with your family and your relationship can withstand pointing out each other's faults.

Having a buddy can be really useful when it comes to the activities in this planner that require concentration and the ability to power through, even when it starts to feel uncomfortable.

If you can't find a buddy, or your don't want to share your Unicorn hunting with anyone, that's totally cool, just find a method of accountability that works for you. It might be setting a deadline, setting alarms as reminders or giving yourself treats or gold stars for completing each step.

Whatever works for you is perfect.

Get organised

To begin this epic adventure we are starting together, we must first get organised. Now, I know for creative types, the idea of being organised is a bit icky, and doesn't feel natural, but I have discovered how important it is when going after your Unicorn. Because Unicorns are a bit resistant to chaos.

To appeal to your creative brain, I have filled this planner with fun illustrations and spaces to fill in that you can customise to however your brain works (lists, mindmaps, sketches, it's all good).

To make it easy for you to flick between sections, you could create your own tabs using washitape, which is how I organise my bullet journal.

To make this journey more fun, I recommend getting yourself some washitape, stickers, coloured pens and highlighters. You might already have plenty of these in your stash, but if not, treat yourself! (Unicorns love treats.) My favourite stickers and washitape come from bujostickers.com.

Magic is the Jam

Many years ago, I was moaning to my partner about the number of how-to books that were flooding the self-help market, that in my opinion, were absolute bullshit. The idea that the author had found a magic bullet, a one-size-fits-all solution to a problem that would help every reader, was utterly preposterous.

Because there are so many factors at play. The reader may have had a completely different upbringing, be in a different country, have different laws they have to abide by, etc. There is no such thing as a one-size-fits-all approach, and in fact, I would go as far as to say that the approach may really only help a few people.

But why is this? Surely it's helpful to share ideas, methods, or strategies that have proven to help the author? Of course it is. But what is not helpful, is to share the desired outcome.

What has occurred is this: the author did a bunch of things, we'll call them ABC. As a result of doing ABC, they received the outcome of XYZ. Excited by their success, they then write a book, that states - Hey! If you do ABC (like I did) then you'll get XYZ! (like me!) And that is where these books become bullshit.

What if you are not meant to get XYZ? What if you are meant to get something bigger? Better? Smaller? (Which might be better for you?)

For me, by promising a particular outcome, you have killed THE MAGIC IN THE MIDDLE. (Which was the title of a book I thought about writing, but I'm basically sharing the whole concept right here for you.)

Quite simply, MAGIC IS THE JAM. If you do the actions, then allow the magic to do its thing, then you will receive the outcome that is perfectly created just for you. If you do the actions, and hope that you get exactly the same result as the author of the book, or as a friend who did the same thing, then in all likelihood, you will be disappointed. And nothing kills magic faster than disappointment.

So as you proceed with this book, remember that the outcomes you receive are perfect for you, and I am not promising you anything* that you may read in the examples or the case studies, but I am promising that if you are willing, committed and ready to make changes, then your Unicorns will be galloping to your door to take you for a magical ride. (Or not, you know, cos I can't control your Unicorns any more than I can control the weather.**)

*Disclaimer: I'm *really* not promising you anything. I am not, and this book is not, responsible for your successes or failures. You are. So own it. (And don't blame me, either way.)

**Okay, so sometimes I can control the weather, but it takes a lot of concentration...

Let it goooo

Many spiritual peeps preach the art of letting go. The practice of non-attachment. Of releasing the need.

None of these things come naturally to us. They are an art, and a practice. And the trickiest part of all? We cannot let go, or release, or become non-attached, with the intention that we're only doing it so it will come back to us, or that it will bring us what we want. We have to genuinely let go. Release. Be non-attached.

It's harder than it sounds. Because as soon as you make the link in your mind, and you think - hey! All I have to do is give that person space, and let go, and they will then come back to me and we'll live happily ever after - it's unlikely that it will happen that way.

Why? Because you're not really letting go. You're pretending to. You ARE attached to a preferred outcome. Basically, you've killed the magic.

When you tie your actions (any actions, not just letting go), to a specific outcome, then you are killing all of the many magical possibilities that may have sprung from those actions.

What if you genuinely let go of a relationship, set the person free, moved on, and actually found a much better relationship?

The possibilities are endless and limitless, but the moment

you slap an outcome on them, or have a sneaky ulterior motive for doing something, you narrowly reduce the possibilities down to very few.

Not much fun, huh?

So how on earth do you let go, fully, completely and genuinely, when you have the thought in the back of your mind that it's not really goodbye?

Ah, well, that's the question isn't it.

Because in a way, the moment you become aware of such thoughts, it becomes very difficult to do. I know when I have let go, completely, with no intention of what I'm letting go coming back to me - it always has.

Yet when I do a sneaky letting go, when I think, I'll just SAY I'm letting go, and ACT like I'm letting go, but not REALLY let go, it never works out very well.

Because you cannot trick the universe. It knows all. Sees all. Feels all. And it acts accordingly.

So remember this, because when you get to the part of manifesting your Unicorn (later in the book), once you have played your part in bringing it into your life, you need to let go of the outcome, let go of the hows of it all, and let the magic do the work.

Dream or Delusion?

Is there a difference? Does it matter? Here's my take.

A dream is an attainable Unicorn. A delusion is an unattainable Unicorn. So, if you dream of being an astronaut, or ballet dancer, or a pro-athlete, but you haven't been training for it your whole life, you don't have the physical requirements, or you're not actually willing to put in the hours of hard work, then it's not a dream. It's a delusion. It's an unattainable Unicorn.

If you dream of being an author, a mother, a marathon runner, an artist, or a doctor, and you have the skills or talent, are willing to put in the hard work, do the training, learn what you need to, then it is an attainable Unicorn. Because it's completely in the realms of possibility in your reality.

There are times where the lines between dreams and delusions blur, and that could look like the person who wants to be a chef, but not just any chef, a Michelin star chef with their own restaurant. Not impossible, but depending on their circumstances, could be a delusion. Or the person who wants to be a best-selling author and make billions. Again, a certain level of delusion, because the number of authors who have achieved this is so few.

But what I have discovered, is that sometimes, the delusions of grandeur serve as motivation and help to keep you going while pursuing your Unicorn, so in actual fact, they are damned handy.

I didn't understand this until I used EFT to get rid of mine. I didn't want to be deluded, I didn't want to look foolish, and be the crazy author who thought that she was going to be rich, selling millions of books and having them made into movies. I think the reason I didn't want to look ridiculous, is because I'd had those dreams for many years, and they had still yet to come to pass. And they were starting to feel impossible. So I decided to get rid of delusions altogether.

But what I hadn't considered was that my delusions were not necessarily impossible, and they were, in fact, the thing that drove me. That made me blog. Made me do live videos, made me go on live Morning TV and talk about angels, and aliens; and appear in a national newspaper, wearing angel wings and talking about my astral travel. My delusions inspired me to keep slugging away, keep writing more books, and keep growing my body of work and readership.

So when I got rid of my delusions, I also got rid of my dreams, and since then, my book sales tanked, my marketing became non-existent, and my attention was diverted onto other things like my hobbies and regular jobs, in other words, more realistic endeavours.

WTF eh?

I never meant to get rid of my dreams. After all, unless you dream big, unless you imagine the seemingly impossible, then it will never happen. And though the chances may be slim, it does happen, but only for those who are deluded enough to think it will. So if you need grand delusions to motivate you, that's totally fine.

They're powerful magic.

However, if you have delusions that are entirely unattainable, then I would recommend releasing them back into the wild, because they are no longer Unicorns, they are mere scapegoats. Excuses for not living your life to its fullest. Release the unattainable Unicorns, and replace them with attainable ones.

Because Unicorns are not goats.

Finding Mojo

Ah, the ever elusive mojo. It's funny, it was only very recently that I discovered what *mojo* actually means. Here is the definition -

>a magic charm, talisman, or spell.
>influence, especially magic power.

Mojo literally means magic, the spark, joy, enthusiasm, your joy de vivre. And at times on this magical Unicorn ride, you will likely misplace yours. Goodness knows it feels like mine has run off on many occasions. And on these occasions, simply getting dressed, having a shower and keeping my stomach from grumbling takes such a huge effort, that I cannot even consider looking for Unicorns.

And you know what? That's okay. Because we can't be sparkling and bubbly all the time.

What's not okay, is to think that mojo is something that is outside of ourselves. Your mojo, your magic, is within. All the time. It just hides sometimes.

Just as the stars still shine, even when it's cloudy, your mojo is there. All you need to do is find a way to clear the clouds, to call the mojo forth. The way to do this might literally be wearing an item of clothing, a piece of jewellery, or having a talisman of some kind. (It might be good to have a few different ones, in case you misplace the physical item.) It might be a song, a piece of music, or a scent that sparks your mojo. Or there might be a phrase that sparks that flame within you, makes you get up, get your Unicorn hunting gear on, and JFDI.

Currently, I have the softest, fluffiest rainbow scarf that is helping me write this. But previously it has been a song that inspires me and gets me raring to go, or a ring or a bracelet. So go find your magic charm, your talisman, imbue it with the power to call forth your mojo when you are feeling low or listless, and then let's get started.

Let the
Hunt
begin!

The Unicorn Process

It's now time to do the work. And hopefully, this planner is laid out in a way that makes it fun, easy and super straightforward. For those of you who like to know what's coming, here is a summary of the Unicorn Process -

- 🔴 Step 1 – Why?
- 🟠 Step 2 – What?
- 🟡 Step 3 – What?
- 🟢 Step 4 – Why?
- 🔵 Step 5 – Buh bye!
- 🟣 Step 6 – Plan
- 🌸 Step 7 – Action!

See? Simple!

Now turn the page, grab your pens and get stuck in. There is no better time than right now. (Because now is all that exists, if you want to get all woo about it.)

STEP 1 – WHY?
Why are you looking for Unicorns?

If you have decided that there is more to life than just eating, sleeping and working, and you are choosing to venture down this path of exploring your dreams and passions, chances are, you are not an ordinary person.

You are likely to be a curious soul, who wishes to experience more joy in their lives, and to discover new and awesome things. You are not content to just eat, sleep, work, and then shuffle off this mad planet we currently call home.

You want to find your Unicorn. You want the epic rainbows after the storm. You want to dance with the faeries and laugh with the leprechaun and ride dragons.

You want to truly LIVE, and not just exist. You want to THRIVE, not merely survive. You want MAGIC, not the mundane.

But Unicorns can be tricky creatures. They are a bit elusive at times and can be fickle too. You have to really want them in your lives in order to find them. If you just talk about finding them, fantasize about finding them, complain they aren't in your life, but all the while, you are not willing to actually step outside your door and go looking for them, then you will never experience the rush of the wind in your hair as you ride them.

So the first step to finding them, is knowing WHY you are looking for them in the first place.

In the first section, under the handy title

Why am I looking for Unicorns?

I want you to answer some or all of the following questions, you decide what's relevant.

What will I FEEL when I get my Unicorn?

What will getting my Unicorn GIVE me?

What will my life be like?

What will my AVERAGE DAY be like?

Do I believe that having my Unicorn will make me feel HAPPIER?

Will it make me wealthier? Sexier? More popular? Funnier?

What do I not have now, that my Unicorn will provide or make possible?

What is missing from my life?

You can write this in list form, in sketches, in bubbles like a mindmap, whatever floats your boat. Make sure you do that now on the next page before reading on. There's several pages in this section, so you can repeat this process over and over with different Unicorns.

It might be good to date the Unicorns, so that in several weeks, months or years, you can look back and see how long it took you to find your Unicorn. You may find that the more practice you get, the faster you get at finding them.

Why am I looking for Unicorns?

January 2022

When I get my unicorns, I will feel:

happy   Contented   fulfilled
           Playful
excited   joyful

my unicorns will give me:
time   peace of mind   happiness
fun   stability   security

Why am I looking for Unicorns?

Why am I looking for Unicorns?

Why am I looking for Unicorns?

Why am I looking for Unicorns?

Why am I looking for Unicorns?

Why am I looking for Unicorns?

Why is the Why important?

When I first set this exercise as the first step in the process, it wasn't with a fully conscious reason. Even though I was asking myself and the workshop participants WHY they wanted their Unicorns, it wasn't fully obvious to me WHY this was important.

During a live online session, it suddenly occurred to me why the WHY was important, and why so many self-help and self-development people have been banging on about the WHY for so long.

It's all to do with vibration.

You cannot attract into your life something you are not. (Bear with me if you are not interested in anything spiritual or alternative, I promise that this is really REALLY helpful to understand, whether you believe in it or not.)

So you cannot attract love into your life if there is none there to begin with. You cannot attract money into your life if there is none there to begin with. You cannot create abundance from a place of lack, etc. Because the Universe brings you what you ARE, what you FEEL and what you AFFIRM. Therefore, wanting something means that you ARE lacking it, you FEEL desperate for it, and you keep AFFIRMING it's not yours yet. So the universe will bring you more lack, desperation and not having it. Because that's what you are projecting.

So the purpose of this exercise, is to find out what you think you will gain from finding your Unicorn, so you can see where you *already have* that thing. So that you know you ARE that thing, you FEEL that thing, and you AFFIRM that thing to be true.

To make that make more sense, I will use an actual example, not just concepts.

Rebecca wants to be an actor. She has wanted to be one since she was a child, but has never had the encouragement or confidence to go for it. But she's now in her 30s, and has decided enough is enough, she wants to pursue her Unicorn. When asked WHY she wants to be an actor, she writes down the following:

When I am an actor, I will feel like I am fulfilling my purpose, I will be creating a legacy, and I when I am working on movies I will be creating financial stability for myself and my family. I will feel excited by my work and will be challenged and pushed beyond my comfort zone. I will be using my talents and strengths and others will be proud of me.

So the things Rebecca sees herself gaining from being an actor are

- A sense of purpose
- Creating a legacy
- Financial stability
- Feeling excited
- Being challenged
- Using her talents

- Using her strengths
- Getting praise from others

So where does Rebecca ALREADY HAVE all those things?

Rebecca feels a sense of purpose when she is writing, as she likes to write articles for a local magazine about parenting. She has created a legacy in that she has two children who are encouraged to explore their own creativity and purpose. She has financial stability from the regular paycheck in her current job, and she feels excited when a new movie comes out featuring her favourite actors. She is challenged by working full time and raising her children with her husband, while still trying to pursue her own passions. She also uses her talents as an actor when reading bedtime stories to her children and doing the voices of the characters. She receives praise from the readers of the magazine, and from her children for making their costumes for school plays.

Now those feelings and emotions might all be in a very different format to how Rebecca wishes to experience them, but they will be on the SAME VIBRATION.

So in order to attract more of those things, Rebecca needs to focus on what she already has.

You cannot build on a void of lack. But you can build on a foundation made from the same vibration.

Have I lost you? I hope not, because this is quite an important part. Put simply, to experience more abundance, seek to find where you already have abundance, and focus on that. As many authors and speakers have already said, what you focus on GROWS. If you wish to experience more stability, focus on the stability you already have. If you wish to experience more love… you know the score.

So read back through your answers to the questions about why you are seeking Unicorns, pick out the core things that you wish to have more of in your life, then consider where you already have those things, and then write them down next to the original points. Get into the *feeling* of each thing. And then get excited. Because if those things are already in your life, then it'll be so easy to attract more of them.

You could also plan to do more of the things that create those feelings, and then really bask in them as you do so.

Where do I already have that?

January 2022

happy — when with my best friend.

contented — when I have clean sheets on the bed

excited — when a new book by a favourite author is released

fulfilled — by my volunteer work

playful — when making things

joyful — when I've made cookies.

time — I have time before bed to read a book.

fun — walking the dog with my friend.

stability — my parents are always there for me.

security — my mum pension.

peace of mind — I know I can handle anything.

happiness — when I cuddle my dog.

Where do I already have that?

Where do I already have that?

Where do I already have that?

Where do I already have that?

Where do I already have that?

Where do I already have that?

STEP 2 – WHAT?

What Unicorns have you already found?

In the second part of step one, we looked at where you already had the feelings and things you wish to have more of. We are now going to look at what Unicorns you have already created and experienced in your life.

So often, we are so focussed on where we are going, or where we want to be, that we forget to truly consider where we have been, and to appreciate and celebrate it. We can want something for months or years, then when it finally arrives, we go:

'Oh, cool, it's here. What's next?'

And that's quite fucking disappointing to the Unicorn who has just arrived. Where's the fireworks? The celebration dinner? The happy dance? The WHOOP! of joy?

Unicorns love a good party. So let's not disappoint them!

Celebrating what you have already created in your life up to now, sets the tone for what you will create.

So on the pages titled -

Unicorns I have already found

I want you to list all the Unicorns you have manifested, created, and received, even if they are no longer with you, and were just passing by. If lists don't turn you on, create a mindmap, do little drawings, whatever gets your creativity flowing.

Look at all areas of your life - what have you already created or manifested? Big or small, significant or insignificant - all Unicorns matter. Write down as many as you can think of.

Some questions to ponder if you are struggling to think of any.

What do you love about your life?

What are your achievements?

What experiences have you had?

What are you proud of?

What would you fight dragons to protect?

What makes you happy?

Where have you travelled to?

What have you received?

What have you given away?

Who have you helped?

What have you created?

Pick two or three of the Unicorns you just wrote down and celebrate them. That's right. Put this book down and do a happy dance, or book a dinner out, or treat yourself to something shiny. Whatever way feels good to celebrate, do it right now. Of course, if you're in a public place, this might be a bit tricky, but do SOMETHING that says to those Unicorns - I am so grateful to have you, I love you, and I want you and the universe to know that! In fact, on the page titled -

Celebration Ideas

- I want you to write down all the ways you would like to celebrate your Unicorns. Then when the occasion arises, you can look at this list for inspiration!

In the future, don't wait until you are riding the Unicorn to celebrate it - act on the INSPIRATION OF CELEBRATION when it occurs - even if that celebratory feeling comes when the Unicorn is merely an idea. Because it is in that moment of excitement that the seed of the Unicorn grows stronger, and is more likely to manifest than if you say - I will wait until it's REAL. Because as we have already discussed, when it's finally really here, you will be too busy looking at the next shiny Unicorn to celebrate it.

Hopefully it will be clear to you from this exercise that you are already an amazing Unicorn finder, so you can be confident that you will find ANY Unicorn you seek, even if it appears to be elusive.

Over the next few days, as you notice more Unicorns in your life that you have manifested, add them to the list, and add new Unicorns to the list as they arrive.

Celebration Ideas

What Unicorns have I already found?

January 2022

I have travelled to five countries.

I have two very good friends.

I have a lovely, warm, safe home.

I have a car that I love driving

I have learned to love myself more

What Unicorns have I already found?

What Unicorns have I already found?

What Unicorns have I already found?

What Unicorns have I already found?

What Unicorns have I already found?

What Unicorns have I already found?

STEP 3 – WHAT

What Unicorns would you like?

You may have many Unicorns that you would love to manifest or bring into your experience, and it's good to explore all possibilities, so first, let's list them all. Look at the following areas your Unicorns might belong to:

Health / Finances / Home / Relationships / Career / Dreams

On the pages with the heading -

Unicorns I would like

- create a mindmap or list of Unicorns in each area, writing down as many as you want. Be as detailed or as general as you wish, and make sure you write down Unicorns that really excite you and make you smile, and especially the ones you think are far too magical and sparkly for you.

Here are some questions to help you figure out what you want:

What did you love doing as a child?

What did you want to be when you grew up?

What could you do for hours and not get bored?

What would you do for free?

What would you do if money were no object?

What kind of relationship would you have if there were no limitations?

What would you like to feel like?

What excites you?

What makes you happy?

What motivates you?

What are you curious about?

What makes you do a happy dance?

When you have written down every Unicorn you can think of, read through each one, and circle less than ten that you would love to experience next in your life. Then go back through those ten or less and pick just five.

Then go through the five and pick just one.

That Unicorn is now the focus for the rest of this book, so make sure it's the shiniest, sparkliest, most exciting one! (You can do more boring ones at a later date, using this method, but starting off big and shiny will help you to see the process through the first time round.)

It's a lot easier to focus on finding one Unicorn at a time, as you can follow the path to it more easily if you are not distracted by paths leading to other Unicorns. You may feel like an expert Unicorn juggler, but try to pick just one for now. Then on the bottom of the page, write down in huge letters what you Unicorn is.

If you get excited, your heart beats fast and you feel like crying with joy just reading the sentence, then you've picked the right one! Move onto the next step. If you read it and feel meh, please go back and pick another one!

Unicorns I would like

My Unicorn is...

to create a YouTube TV show.

Unicorns I would like

My Unicorn is...

Unicorns I would like

My Unicorn is...

Unicorns I would like

My Unicorn is...

Unicorns I would like

My Unicorn is...

Unicorns I would like

My Unicorn is...

Unicorns I would like

My Unicorn is...

STEP 4 – WHY
Why don't you have it already?

Look at the Unicorn you have chosen, then answer the question:

Why don't I already have it?

There might be lots of reasons why, and though it might feel like a bit of a depressing exercise, we need to get to the root of why it's not already here. So on the pages titled -

Why don't I already have my Unicorn?

- answer as many of the following questions as you can.

Do you believe you deserve it? That you are worthy of it?
Do you believe it is possible for you?
Do you REALLY want it?
Do you think others will think differently of you?
Are you procrastinating?
Are you overwhelmed?
Are there people in your life convinced you won't get it?
Do you love to complain about not having it?

Are you afraid that your fantasy of it is better than the reality might be?
Are you afraid of being disappointed by getting it?
Are you a drama llama who doesn't want a happy life?
Are you afraid to do the work in case it doesn't work?
Are you afraid of getting it and then losing it?
Are you an information junkie who doesn't take action?

I go through all these reasons and more in *Where's My F**king Unicorn?* So have a look through that if you need any more inspiration on why you may be without your Unicorn.

Write down all the reasons or excuses or beliefs why you haven't already got this shiny, glorious Unicorn in your life. Write down how you feel about the Unicorn, what you think about the Unicorn, and what you believe about the Unicorn.

After looking at all the reasons why you don't already have it, do you still want it? Is it still the Unicorn you would like to focus on? Is it still the one that excites you the most right now?

This is no time to be sensible, we want the sparkly Unicorns, not the dull ones! (You can choose to do this process with some more sensible, less shiny Unicorns later, but for this first time, choose a truly fabulous Unicorn.)

Why don't I already have my Unicorn?

January 2022

YouTube TV show.

- need better camera equipment
- need a team to help film.
- need editing software
- internet might be too slow to upload
- the quality might not be good enough
- maybe no one will watch it.
- don't know how to do the technical stuff

Why don't I already have my Unicorn?

Why don't I already have my Unicorn?

Why don't I already have my Unicorn?

Why don't I already have my Unicorn?

Why don't I already have my Unicorn?

Why don't I already have my Unicorn?

Step 5 – buh bye
Clearing the Path to Your Unicorn

The first step in clearing obstacles is understanding the roots of them. So I want you to read through all your reasons why you don't have your Unicorn, and look for the underlying EMOTIONS.

Here are a few possibilities to help you identify what's hidden beneath. Write the emotion next to each excuse/reason, or tick the list below, or write your own list on the next pages.

Fear
Anger
Unworthy
Shame
Embarrassment
Self-Doubt
Guilt
Frustration
Lack
Despair
Envy
Hopelessness
Apathy

Afraid
Useless
Unloved
Alone
Depressed
Discouraged
Fatigued
Inferior
Humiliated
Incapable
Indecisive
Under-qualified
Powerless
Overwhelmed
Resentful
Sceptical
Uncertain
Terrified

Once you have identified the emotions and written them down, we are going to release them, and in doing so, hopefully release the excuses from your life, so you can go get those Unicorns with wild abandon! (And glee. Lots of glee.)

Emotions blocking the Unicorns

lack
embarrassment
incapable
Underqualified
alone
overwhelm
self-doubt.

Emotions blocking the Unicorns

Emotions blocking the Unicorns

Emotions blocking the Unicorns

Emotions blocking the Unicorns

Emotions blocking the Unicorns

Emotions blocking the Unicorns

As described in *Where's My F**king Unicorn?* We are going to use EFT to release those emotions, and if you have a buddy for this wild ride, now is the perfect time for you to get together with your buddy and release these out of your system. It's easier to do this part with a buddy, because often they will see the patterns and will be able to prompt you if you start to feel resistance building up.

So get comfy, pick the first emotion on your list, and begin by tapping on point 1 on your hand. You can remain quiet while tapping, just focussing on the emotion, or if you find it helpful, you can make statements out loud while tapping on each point. If we use fear as an example, and the Unicorn is being a motivational speaker, the statements might sound something like this -

Point.1. Even though I am afraid I will make a fool of myself, I totally love and accept myself.

Pt. 2. Even though I am afraid no one will come to my talks, and I will be embarrassed, I totally love and accept myself.

Pt. 3. Even though I feel I have something to share, I'm afraid it won't be well received, and others will think I am ridiculous, I totally love and accept myself

Pt. 4. Even though I'm afraid I will be judged for my experiences in life, I totally love and accept myself.

Pt. 5. Even though I'm afraid I will get too nervous and will mess up on stage, I totally love and accept myself.

Pt. 6 - Pt. 8 - Keep stating any feelings of fear that arise as you talk, often things will pop up that you weren't consciously aware of. When you get to Pt. 8, go back to Pt. 2 and keep cycling Pts 2 to 8 until you run out of negatives.

Then, you can move onto neutral statements, like:

- I know I have something worth sharing that might help people.

- I think I would enjoy speaking to groups of people.

Then when you feel able to, move onto positive statements of what you would like to feel, such as:

- I love standing on stage and sharing my message.

- I love helping people with my stories.

- I love sharing my knowledge.

- I love sharing my passion for my subject.

Do this process with each emotion/feeling, but **don't do them all in one session**. Do a few to begin with, and if it feels like too much, take a break. You might feel triggered by what arises, you might find yourself crying, or angry, or annoyed. If so, tap on the emotions that arise from the process too. This is where having a buddy helps, because they can be your anchor, to ground you while you process. You can spread this section out over the course of a week, or a couple of weeks, to allow things to settle inbetween. You are reprogramming old beliefs and thoughts that you have had for decades, so it is going to have an effect on you. Take your time on this part.

If you need someone to guide you through it but don't have a buddy, search on YouTube for a video that relates to the right emotion or missing Unicorn. Follow the video, then come back here.

After tapping on all the emotions, sit for a moment and think about your Unicorn. Do you feel any resistance? Do you still feel it's not possible? Are the excuses rising up? Or are you feeling excited about finding it? About experiencing it?

If you feel those excuses are still affecting you, can you at least own them? Can you admit to being a drama llama? Can you see the positives in being an information junkie? Can you laugh at making all your decisions based on whether or not mercury is in retrograde?

Owning your shit gives it less power over your life, and therefore no longer holds you back from getting your fucking Unicorn. And often, once you own your shit, it actually completely disappears.

Before you move on to the next step, I want you to celebrate. Pick something from your celebration ideas list, and do it. Celebrate taking things into your own hands, empowering yourself and making the effort (because tapping on your emotions does take a lot of mental effort) to change your life.

You are no longer just wishing your life were different. You are DOING SOMETHING about it. And that is a huge thing that requires celebration.

So please, before you move on, celebrate now.

STEP 6 – Plan
Making a Unicorn Plan

Now I have a confession to make here. I hate planning. I hate deciding on things that will happen in the future. I hate plotting books, or figuring out the whole journey before taking a step, because I just enjoy going with the flow and seeing where it takes me. But I have realised, on this Unicorn journey, that making a plan is essential if I want to get certain Unicorns.

What is not essential, is working out every tiny detail of the path to the Unicorn, because as discussed in **Magic is the Jam,** that would kill the magic. After all, the HOW is not up to us, it's up to the Universe (God/Source, etc.). All we need to do is to work out WHAT we want, and the HOW takes cares of itself.

BUT...

We DO need to take action. We DO need to move toward our Unicorn and show the universe that we really do want it, that we are willing to meet it partway. And then, we can allow the magical jam to do its thing.

Which means we need to make a plan. But this is not a step by step plan, this is not a detailed plan. This is a next tiny step plan.

Have a think about what could you do that would move you closer to your Unicorn. What action could you take right now, or this week or month, that would bring it closer to your reality?

On the page titled **My Unicorn Plan**, create a mindmap with your Unicorn in the centre, and then ideas of the next possible step surrounding it. Here are some ideas to get you going.

You could:

Research the idea

Look up prices/costs/fees

Make a phone call

Send an email

Write a proposal

Write the opening lines of the book

Create a plot

Buy materials/instruments/tools/equipment, etc.

Book a class/course

Sketch the outline of the idea

Write down as many possible next steps as you can, even the ones you don't feel ready for, or can't afford, or think are impossible.

Please Note:

Depending on how supportive your immediate family are, it might be best to keep your Unicorn plans to yourself for now, and if you need support or cheering on, try to seek it from your Unicorn seeking friends, or your buddy, as they will encourage you in your endeavours, rather than try to stop you.

My Unicorn Plan

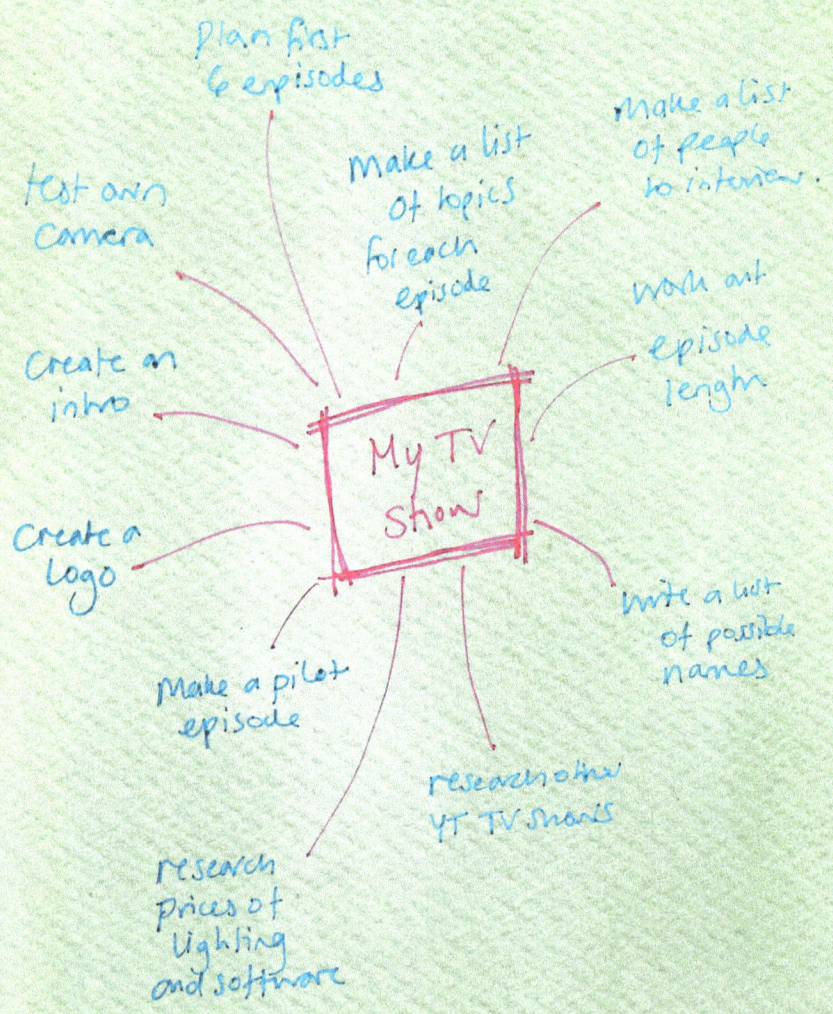

My Unicorn Plan

My Unicorn Plan

My Unicorn Plan

My Unicorn Plan

My Unicorn Plan

STEP 7 – ACTION

Look through all of those possible steps, and pick one. Do it now. You heard me. **RIGHT NOW.**

Because NOW is all there is. And if you are serious about bringing this Unicorn into your life, then there really is no time like the present. So what are you waiting for?

NOW.

RIGHT *NOW*.

STOP READING AND *DO IT NOW*.

Still feeling resistance? Get tapping again. Tap on the resistance, tap on the fear, tap on whatever comes to mind when you think about taking this first step. Then when you feel like it has gone, DO IT NOW.

HAVE YOU DONE IT?

I don't care what time of day it is, I don't care if you're tired, **DO IT NOW.**

Taking action is one of the most powerful tools in our manifesting box. It shows the universe and the people around us that we are actually fucking serious. But of course, we can be serious and still have fun along the way! I find plenty of stickers helps with that! And snacks. Lots of snacks.

If you really can't take action right this minute (because you are reading this on the toilet or in the bath), when will you take action? Set a deadline, write it down. Then ask someone to hold you accountable, who will check that you actually did do it. Or set an alarm on your phone to remind you to do it.

Then once you have taken that action, **CELEBRATE.**

You just took a step towards bringing your Unicorn into your life! Celebrate every step, and then be sure to enjoy riding the Unicorn when it arrives, but remember, the journey to get to it is just as important, if not more important, than the Unicorn itself.

Brainstorm ways to celebrate, add them to your celebration list, and make a promise to your accountability buddy to celebrate each step.

Then OWN your success along the way. You deserve every bit of it.

Hopefully, taking that one action will inspire you (because it was actually a lot easier than you thought, huh?) and you will pick another action, and do that. Then another, then another.

Before you know it, you are well underway to getting your Unicorn. Be open to signs and synchronicities, to people offering support or help, to opportunities popping up, money becoming available, and your Unicorn getting closer to you.

Celebrate everything good that happens to bring you closer. (Hint, it's ALL good.)

At this point, feel free to go back to your list of Unicorns and pick another one. Then repeat the process from steps 4 to 7. Or wait for this Unicorn to manifest, before starting a new one. It all depends on how many Unicorns you can handle at once!

You
fucking
did it!

Wasn't that fun??

So that's it. The Unicorn Process. Now, hopefully you have actually done the activities, and the EFT as you went through, and you haven't just read this book only to set it aside, because as I said at the beginning of the book, simply reading my words will not change your life.

But doing the activities and taking action, just might. And even if it doesn't, what have you got to lose? (Except some outdated beliefs and fears?)

You can apply the steps to as many Unicorns as you want, just keep repeating the steps, and keep tapping on the emotions or feelings that are holding you back, and before you know it, you will be riding all your Unicorns and having a fucking brilliant time.

Please do let me know how you get on, you can get in touch with me via Instagram - @michellegordonauthor - or email - theamethystangel@hotmail.co.uk.

About the Author

As well as writing books, Michelle has a busy publishing business, and runs a letterpress studio and shop. In her spare (!!) time, she loves to knit, sew, crochet, walk her doggo in the woods and meet up with her fabulous friends.

Michelle loves to hear from readers, so if you would like to get in touch, email her at theamethystangel@hotmail.co.uk or on Instagram - @michellegordonauthor

Please do leave a review for this workbook wherever you bought a copy! Thanks!

michellegordon.co.uk

www.ingramcontent.com/pod-product-compliance
Lightning Source LLC
Chambersburg PA
CBHW041302240426
43661CB00010B/997